SANDWICHES

SANDWICHES

SARAH TYSON HESTON RORER

9 789389 582673

ISBN: 978-93-89582-67-3

First Published: -

LECTOR HOUSE LLP
E-MAIL: lectorpublishing@gmail.com

SANDWICHES

BY

MRS. S. T. RORER

Author of Mrs. Rorer's New Cook Book, Philadelphia Cook Book, Bread and
Bread-Making, and other Valuable Works on Cookery.

REVISED AND ENLARGED EDITION

CONTENTS

Page

SANDWICHES

SWEET SANDWICHES

CANAPÉS

SCENTED SANDWICHES

SANDWICHES

Sandwiches may be made from one of three or four kinds of bread; whole wheat bread, Boston brown or oatmeal bread, white bread and rye bread made into square, deep loaves; in fact, all bread used for sandwiches should be made especially for the purpose, so that the slices may be in good form, and sufficiently large to cut into fancy shapes.

The butter may be used plain, slightly softened or it may be seasoned and flavored with just a suspicion of paprika, a little white pepper, and a few drops of Worcestershire sauce.

For ordinary sandwiches use the bread without toasting. For canapés, toast is to be preferred. Sandwiches are principally used for buffet lunches or evening sociables, where only a light, substantial lunch is required. In these days they are made in great varieties. Almost all sorts of meat, if properly seasoned, may be made into delicious sandwiches. If the meat is slightly moistened with cream or olive oil, sandwiches for traveling, provided each one is carefully wrapped in oiled paper, will keep fresh three or four days. The small French rolls may have the centres scooped out, the spaces filled with chicken salad or chopped oysters, and served as sandwiches. The rolls may be made especially for that purpose, not more than two inches long and one and a half inches wide; with coffee, they make an attractive meal easily served.

Ordinary sandwiches may be made either square, triangular, long, narrow, round or crescent shaped. One slice of bread will usually make one round sandwich and one crescent, provided the cutting is done economically. Meat used for sandwiches should be chopped very fine and slightly moistened with cream, melted butter, olive oil or mayonnaise dressing well seasoned. Fish should be rubbed or pounded in a mortar; add enough sauce tartare to make it sufficiently moist to easily spread.

Turkey, chicken, game, tongue, beef and mutton, with their proper seasonings, moistened with either mayonnaise or French dressing, make exceedingly nice sandwiches.

TO KEEP SANDWICHES

It is frequently necessary to make sandwiches several hours before they are needed. As they dry quickly they must be carefully wrapped or they will be unpalatable. Wring from cold water two ordinary tea towels; put one on top of the other. An old tablecloth will answer the purpose very well. As fast as the sandwiches are made put them on top of the damp towel; when you have the desired quantity, cover the top with moist lettuce leaves; fold over the towels, and put outside of this a perfectly dry, square cloth. Sandwiches will keep in this way for several hours, and in perfectly good condition. On a very warm day they may be covered all over with moist lettuce leaves; use the green ones that are not so palatable or sightly for garnishing.

BREAD

To make good sandwiches, especially when one is a long way from a city, it is quite necessary to know how to make sandwich bread, which is quite different, or should be, from ordinary bread. Compressed yeast is always to be preferred, but if one cannot get it, the next best is good home-made yeast. Bread for sandwiches must be baked in rather large square pans, and must be just a little lighter and softer than bread for the table. The following recipes will, I am sure, help the "out of town" housewife. Nut bread is usually made into simple bread and butter sandwiches; the nuts in the bread are quite sufficient filling.

YEAST

4 good sized potatoes
1 quart of boiling water
2 tablespoonfuls of sugar
1 tablespoonful of salt

Pare and grate the potatoes into the hot water, stir over the fire until it reaches boiling point, and simmer gently for five minutes. Take from the fire, add the sugar and salt, and when lukewarm add a cupful of yeast, or two dry yeast cakes that have been moistened in a little water, or one cake of compressed yeast. Turn the mixture into a jar and cover with a saucer. Stir it down as fast as it comes to the top of the jar. When it falls, or ceases to be very light, which will be five or six hours, pour it into a bottle, put the cork in very loosely and stand it in a cold place. Use one cupful of this to each two loaves of bread.

GERMAN POTATO BREAD

Boil one potato until tender; mash it through a sieve, add to it a half pint of warm water and a teaspoonful of sugar. Stir in one cupful of flour and one cupful of yeast; let this stand for two hours, or until very light. It is better to make this at seven o'clock, so the bread may be sponged at nine or ten. Scald a pint of milk, add to it a pint of water, beat in a quart and a pint of flour. The batter should be thick enough to drop, rather than pour from the spoon. Then stir in the potato starter, and stand in a place about 65° Fahr. over night. Next morning knead thoroughly, adding flour. Put this aside until very light, about two hours, then mold into loaves, put it into square greased pans, and when light bake in a moderately quick oven three-quarters of an hour.

This recipe will make two box loaves and a dozen rolls.

NINETEENTH CENTURY BREAD

Scald a pint of milk, add a pint of water, a teaspoonful of salt, and when lukewarm, one compressed yeast cake moistened in a little warm water. Add sufficient whole wheat flour to make a batter, beat thoroughly, cover and stand aside two and a half hours; then stir, adding more whole wheat flour until you have a dough. Knead quickly, separate into loaves, put each in a square greased pan, cover and stand in a warm place about one hour, until very light. Slash the top with a sharp knife, brush with water and bake in a moderate oven three-quarters of an hour.

WHITE BREAD

Add a pint of water to a pint of scalded milk; when lukewarm add one compressed yeast cake, moistened, and a teaspoonful of salt. Add sufficient flour gradually, beating all the while, to make a dough. Knead this dough until it is soft and elastic, and free from stickiness. Put it into a greased bowl, stand it in a warm place three hours. Separate it into loaves, knead five minutes, put the loaves in square greased pans and stand aside until very light. Slash the top with a sharp knife, brush with water, and bake in a moderate oven three-quarters of an hour. This should make two loaves, or a dozen bread sticks and a dozen rolls.

NUT BREAD

1 quart of flour
4 level teaspoonfuls of baking powder
1 teaspoonful of salt
1 cupful of chopped nuts
1½ cupfuls of milk

Add the baking powder and salt to the flour and sift them. Add the nuts, mix thoroughly and gradually add the milk. Knead this into a loaf, put it into a square pan, brush the top with melted butter, let it stand twenty minutes, and bake in a moderate oven three-quarters of an hour.

ANCHOVY SANDWICHES

Beat a quarter of a pound of butter to a cream, adding gradually two tablespoonfuls of lemon juice, a saltspoonful of paprika, two tablespoonfuls of anchovy paste. Spread this on thin slices of bread, put two together, trim off the crusts, and cut into triangles.

ANCHOVY AND EGG SANDWICHES

Mash the yolks of four hard-boiled eggs with two tablespoonfuls of melted butter or olive oil, add a half teaspoonful of salt, a dash of paprika and a tablespoonful of anchovy paste or two mashed anchovies. Spread this between thin slices of buttered bread, press the slices together, trim off the crusts and cut into triangles.

Sardines may be used in the place of anchovies.

COLD BEEF SANDWICHES

Take the remains of cold roasted beef, and chop very fine; put it into a bowl; to each half pint of meat, add a half teaspoonful of salt, a tablespoonful of tomato catsup, a teaspoonful of Worcestershire sauce and a teaspoonful of melted butter; work this together. Cut the crust from the ends of a loaf of whole wheat bread; butter lightly and slice; so continue until you have the desired number of slices; spread the slices with a layer of the seasoned meat; put two slices together, and cut into desired shapes.

CAVIAR SANDWICHES NO. 1

Beat a quarter of a pound of butter to a cream; add two tablespoonfuls of onion juice, the same of lemon, a saltspoonful of paprika, and gradually four tablespoonfuls of caviar. Spread this on thin slices of brown bread or pumpernickel, put two together, press lightly and cut into long, narrow shapes.

CAVIAR SANDWICHES NO. 2

Cut slices of bread in crescent-shaped pieces, butter one side and toast. Have ready two hard-boiled eggs, remove yolks, put them through sieve, chop whites very fine, and spread toast with layer of caviar; then sprinkle over first a little of whites, then a little of the yolks of the eggs. Put over in the form of a ring a piece of onion, the onion having first been cut into thin slices, and then separated.

CELERY SANDWICHES

Cut slices of bread, butter one side and toast. Cut the white part of celery into thin slices, cover it over the bread, then cover this with a layer of mayonnaise dressing, cover with another piece of toast, cut into squares and serve. All sandwiches of this kind must be used as soon as made.

CELERY SALAD SANDWICHES

Put four eggs into warm water; bring to the boiling point, and keep there, without boiling, for fifteen minutes. Take the white portion from one head of celery; wash and chop it very fine. Remove the shells from the hard-boiled eggs, and either chop them very fine or put through a vegetable press, and mix with them the celery; add a half teaspoonful of salt and a dash of pepper. Butter the bread before you cut it from the loaf. After you have a sufficient quantity cut, put over each slice a layer of the mixed egg and celery; put right in the center of this a teaspoonful of mayonnaise dressing, and sort of smooth it all over. Put two pieces together and press them lightly. Trim off the crusts, and cut the sandwiches into pieces about two inches wide and the length of the slices.

ROLLED BREAD AND BUTTER SANDWICHES

Beat the butter to a cream. Remove the crusts from the loaf, butter each slice before you cut it off, and roll at once. These may be tied with narrow baby ribbon or wrapped at once in waxed paper, fringing and twisting the ends.

ROLLED CHICKEN SANDWICHES

Trim the crusts from the entire loaf, butter each slice and cut it off as thin as possible; spread it quickly with the mixture, roll and wrap it at once in waxed paper. If the bread is home-made and cracks in the rolling, put a colander over a kettle of boiling water, throw in it a few slices at a time, as soon as they have softened spread them with soft butter, then cover with the mixture, roll and wrap in waxed paper.

To make the mixture, chop sufficient cold boiled chicken to make a pint. Rub together two level tablespoonfuls of butter and two of flour, add slowly a half cupful of hot milk, stir over the fire for a minute, then add the chicken, a level teaspoonful of salt, a half teaspoonful of celery seed, a saltspoonful of white pepper, a dash of red pepper, a teaspoonful of onion juice and a grating of nutmeg; mix and cool. This will make four dozen rolled sandwiches.

SANDWICHES À LA RORER

Chop sufficient white meat of cooked chicken to make a half pint. Select two fine bunches of cress, and with a sharp knife shave it very fine. Wash and dry the crisp portion from a head of lettuce. Put the yolks of two eggs into a saucepan, add the juice from two lemons and stir over hot water until the mixture is thick; take from the fire and add slowly two tablespoonfuls of olive oil; add this to the chicken and season with a half teaspoonful of salt and a dash of pepper. Butter a slice of white bread, put over a rather thick layer of the chicken mixture, then a slice of brown bread, buttered on both sides; cover this with a thick layer of cress, dust it lightly with salt and pepper, then another slice of white bread, buttered; press these firmly together, trim the crusts and cut into fingers.

CHICKEN AND ALMOND SANDWICHES

Chop sufficient cold cooked chicken to make a half pint. Chop a quarter of a pound of blanched almonds, add them to the chicken, add four tablespoonfuls of cream, a half teaspoonful of salt and a dash of pepper; mix thoroughly, put between thin slices of buttered bread and cut into crescents or rounds.

CHICKEN AND LETTUCE À LA KENDALL

Put sufficient cold boiled chicken through the meat chopper to make a half pint, pound it in a mortar or rub it in a bowl with the hard-boiled yolks of four eggs, four tablespoonfuls of thick cream, a half teaspoonful of salt, a dash of pepper, and if you have it, two saltspoonfuls of celery seed; in the winter you may add a half cupful of finely chopped celery. Butter thin slices of white bread, cover them with this mixture, place on top a slice of brown bread buttered on both sides, then a thick layer of shredded celery, with a tablespoonful of mayonnaise in the middle, then another slice of buttered white bread; press together, trim the crusts and cut into fingers.

PRINCESS SANDWICHES

Chop sufficient cold chicken to make a half pint, add the juice of half a lemon, two tablespoonfuls of melted butter or olive oil, twelve walnuts chopped very fine, a half teaspoonful of paprika and a half teaspoonful of salt. Put this mixture between thin slices of buttered bread, trim the crusts and cut into fingers.

WINDSOR SANDWICHES

Chop sufficient cold boiled chicken to make a half pint, add a half cupful of finely chopped celery, a half teaspoonful of salt, a dash of pepper and four table-spoonfuls of cream; mix. Chop sufficient cold boiled ham or tongue to make a half pint, add a tablespoonful of tomato catsup, a few drops of Worcestershire sauce and a dash of pepper. Trim the crusts from an entire loaf of bread, butter the end of the loaf and cut off a thin slice, and so continue until you have the desired quantity of bread.

Shred one head of Romaine or a bunch of cress. This of course must be crisp and dry. Put a layer of the chicken mixture on the buttered side of a slice of bread, put on top another slice of buttered bread, then a thick layer of the shredded cress or Romaine. Put a thick layer of the tongue mixture on another slice of bread and cover it over the cress. Press firmly together and cut the slices directly into halves the long way. Wrap in waxed paper or tie with baby ribbon. Served at afternoon teas. If well made, they are the most elaborate and dainty of all sandwiches.

TEA BISCUIT SANDWICHES

Put one quart of flour into a bowl; add four level teaspoonfuls of baking pow-der, a teaspoonful of salt, and sift. Rub in two level tablespoonfuls of butter and add sufficient milk to make a dough. This dough must not be soft, but must be sufficiently stiff to handle quickly. Knead quickly and roll into a sheet a quarter of an inch thick. Cut into good-sized round biscuits; they must be at least two and a half to three inches in diameter. Brush them with milk and bake in a quick oven. When done, cut the center from each biscuit, leaving a wall one inch thick; take out the crumb. Fill this space with deviled chicken. Chop sufficient cold cooked chicken to make a pint; add gradually eight tablespoonfuls of melted butter, cream or olive oil, a dash of cayenne, a saltspoonful of white pepper, a saltspoonful of celery seed and a saltspoonful of paprika. When thoroughly mixed fill the spaces just even and send at once to the table. These are nice for porch suppers, and may be served with either tea, coffee or chocolate, or may be used as an accompaniment to mayonnaise of tomatoes.

CHEESE SANDWICHES NO. 1

Butter thin slices of pumpernickel or brown bread; put between each two slic-es a very thin layer of Swiss cheese, put two together, and cut into triangles; gar-nish with cress.

CHEESE SANDWICHES NO. 2

Chop fine a quarter of a pound of soft American cheese; put it into a saucepan, add the yolk of one egg beaten with two tablespoonfuls of cream, a saltspoonful of salt, a dash of red pepper and half a teaspoonful of Worcestershire sauce. Have ready cut and buttered a sufficient number of slices of bread, either white or whole wheat. Stir the cheese over the fire until it is thoroughly melted; take from the fire and when cool spread it between the slices of bread and butter; that is, spread it on one slice and cover with the other; press two together and cut into forms.

CHEESE SANDWICHES NO. 3

Rub or pound until perfectly smooth or well mixed one tablespoonful of butter, two tablespoonfuls of soft club-house cheese, a tablespoonful of grated Parmesan, a saltspoonful of salt, and a teaspoonful of anchovy paste; add a teaspoonful of tarragon vinegar and a half saltspoonful of pepper. Cut the bread into thin slices, toast it until it is crisp, not hard; spread this mixture on one slice, cover it with another, and cut into shapes.

WORKMAN'S CHEESE SANDWICHES

Cut slices of brown bread about a half inch thick. Do not remove the crusts. Take a half pint of cottage cheese; press it through a sieve; add to it two tablespoonfuls of melted butter, a half teaspoonful of salt and two tablespoonfuls of thick cream. Beat until smooth and light. Spread each slice of bread thickly with the cheese mixture, then put a very thin slice of white bread on top of the cheese, then cheese and brown bread, press together. Have the outside brown bread with a layer of cheese on each, and between the layers of cheese a slice of white bread. These are palatable, and are very much better for the average workman than bread and ham.

GERMAN SANDWICHES

Put a half pound of Swiss cheese through the meat grinder; add to it the yolks of two eggs, four tablespoonfuls of olive oil, a dash of cayenne and a half teaspoonful of salt. Rub until you have a perfectly smooth paste. Put this mixture between layers of buttered rye bread and serve. Do not trim the crusts nor cut.

HONOLULU SANDWICHES

Put two Spanish sweet peppers (pimientos), one Neufchatel cheese, one pared and quartered apple and twelve blanched almonds through the meat grinder. These may be put through alternately, or mixed as you grind. Rub the mixture, add a half teaspoonful of salt and a saltspoonful of paprika. Spread this between thin slices of buttered white or brown bread. Press, cut the crusts and cut into fingers.

MY FAVORITE

½ pound of American cheese
½ cupful of thick sour cream
1 teaspoonful of Worcestershire sauce
1 tablespoonful of tomato catsup
½ teaspoonful of salt
½ teaspoonful of paprika

Chop or mash the cheese, add gradually the cream, and when smooth add all the other ingredients. Spread this mixture on thin slices of buttered bread, cover the top with chopped cress, then cover with another slice of bread, press the two together, trim off the crusts and cut into triangles.

CREOLE SANDWICHES

Put a half pound of American cheese through your meat grinder, add to it one Neufchatel cheese, mix well together; add one fresh peeled chopped tomato. Peel the tomato and cut it into halves; squeeze out the seeds and chop the flesh quite fine. Add one finely chopped sweet red pepper. Add a half teaspoonful of salt and a little black pepper; mix and spread between slices of white bread, or you may use one slice of white with one slice of whole wheat bread. These are usually served cut into rounds with an ordinary cake cutter. If you cut these economically you can make one good sized round sandwich and a crescent from each, or if you use a very small cutter you should make four round sandwiches.

CURRY SANDWICHES

Rub one Neufchatel or Philadelphia cream cheese to a paste. Add one pimiento, chopped fine; a dozen almonds put through the meat grinder; a dozen pecan meats, also ground; a tablespoonful of tomato catsup, a level teaspoonful of curry and two tablespoonfuls of desiccated grated cocoanut. Mix thoroughly, add sufficient olive oil to make a smooth paste, and spread between thin, unbuttered slices of white bread; trim the crusts and cut into long fingers. These are nice to serve with plain lettuce salad at dinner.

DEVILED CHEESE SANDWICHES

Put one pound of American cheese through your meat chopper. Add two tablespoonfuls of tomato catsup, one teaspoonful of Worcestershire sauce, a half teaspoonful of paprika, a dash of cayenne, two tablespoonfuls of olive oil or melted butter, four tablespoonfuls of sherry and a half teaspoonful of salt. Mix until perfectly smooth, and spread between thin slices of buttered bread; trim the crusts and cut into triangles.

ROQUEFORT SANDWICHES

Mash a quarter of a pound of Roquefort cheese, adding gradually sufficient melted butter to make a paste. Spread this between slices of buttered bread, press together, trim the crusts, and cut into fingers.

CAMEMBERT SANDWICHES

Spread Camembert cheese between slices of buttered whole wheat bread, trim the crusts and cut into shape. These may be served after lunch with coffee, or are exceedingly nice for picnics or for afternoons where coffee is served.

COTTAGE CHEESE SANDWICHES

These are nice for country picnics. The cottage cheese should be made rather dry. After it has drained and is quite dry, moisten it by adding either thick cream or melted butter; do not make it too soft. Add a saltspoonful of black pepper and a palatable seasoning of salt. Spread between slices of buttered whole wheat or white bread, press the two together, trim the crusts and cut into shape.

SALT-CUCUMBER SANDWICHES

Spread the bread, and cut the slices about half an inch thick. Then cut a German or Holland cucumber into very thin slices; put these slices all over the bread. Take the center from a head of lettuce; hold it together, and slice it down in sort of shreds; put this over the cucumber, and have ready some white meat of chicken, cut into the thinnest possible slices, and cover the lettuce with chicken; then sprinkle over more shredded lettuce and a little mayonnaise; put over another slice of buttered bread; press the two together, trim into shape and serve on a napkin in a pretty wicker basket.

CUCUMBER SANDWICHES

These are very nice to serve with a fish course in place of bread or rolls and a salad. Slice the cucumbers very thin and soak them in ice water for one or two hours. They must be crisp and brittle and made just at serving time. Beat together three tablespoonfuls of olive oil, one tablespoonful of vinegar, a saltspoonful of salt and a dash of pepper; stand this dressing on the ice until it thickens. Butter thin slices of bread, cover them with a layer of cucumbers that have been drained and dried on a napkin, sprinkle over the dressing, put on another layer of buttered bread. Press together, trim the crusts and cut into triangles. Heap these at once on a napkin and send to the table.

CURRIED OYSTER SANDWICHES

Butter a slice of bread before you take it off the loaf; cut it about a half inch thick and remove the crusts. First of all, cover each slice with a thin layer of hard-boiled egg that has been pressed through a sieve or chopped very fine. In the center of this sandwich put the soft parts of six pickled oysters. Put a tablespoonful of butter and one of flour into a little saucepan; mix without melting; add a gill of thick cream, a teaspoonful of onion juice and a teaspoonful of curry and a half teaspoonful of turmeric. Bring to boiling point; beat and stand away until perfectly cold. When you are ready to serve the sandwiches, cover each one with a thin layer of this sauce; put a slice of bread on top, press together, and serve. The sauce must not go over the sandwiches until you are ready to serve; and then, remember, you have but one layer between two slices of bread.

CURRIED EGG SANDWICHES

Hard boil four eggs, remove the yolks from the whites; chop the whites very, very fine, and press the yolks through a sieve. Add to the yolks gradually four tablespoonfuls of melted butter or olive oil, a half teaspoonful of salt, a teaspoonful of onion juice, a half teaspoonful of curry, and rub until thoroughly smooth. Spread thin slices of bread, cover them with a very thin layer of the yolk mixture, then a layer of the chopped whites, another slice of buttered bread. Press together, trim the crusts and cut into shapes.

CURRIED SARDINE SANDWICHES

Remove the heads, tails and bones from one large box of sardines. Rub them to a paste, add a tablespoonful of melted butter, a half teaspoonful of curry powder and a saltspoonful of salt. Spread this mixture between slices of buttered bread, press the two together, trim the crusts and cut into shape.

CURRIED CHICKEN SANDWICHES

Chop sufficient cold boiled chicken to make a half pint. Rub together one tablespoonful of butter and one tablespoonful of flour; add a half cupful of cold milk, and stir over hot water until you have a smooth, thick paste. Add the chicken gradually to this, mashing and rubbing all the while. Add a level teaspoonful of curry powder, a half teaspoonful of salt, a teaspoonful of onion juice and a teaspoonful of lemon juice. When cold, spread between layers of buttered bread, trim the crusts and cut into shapes.

Almost any bits of left-over meat may be substituted for the chicken and made into sandwiches of this kind.

CRAB SANDWICHES

Remove the meat from six hard-boiled crabs; mix it with four tablespoonfuls of mayonnaise dressing; put it between slices of bread and butter and press two together; trim off the crusts, cut into triangles and serve at once.

Crab and lobster sandwiches should not be allowed to stand for more than an hour, and then must be wrapped carefully in a clean, damp cloth.

CREAM OF CHICKEN SANDWICHES

Take sufficient white meat of chicken to make a half cup; chop and pound it; reduce it to a paste. Put a teaspoonful of granulated gelatin in two tablespoonfuls of cold water; then stand it over the fire until it has dissolved. Whip a half pint of cream to a stiff froth. Add the gelatin to the chicken; add a teaspoonful of grated horseradish and a half teaspoonful of salt. Stir this until it begins to thicken, cool and add carefully the whipped cream and stand it away until very cold. When ready to make the sandwiches, butter the bread and cut the slices a little thicker than the usual slices for sandwiches. Cover each slice with this cream mixture; trim off the crusts and cut sandwiches into fancy shapes. Garnish the top with olives cut into rings. In the center of each sandwich make just a little mound of capers, using the olives at the four corners; each sandwich may be garnished in a different way. Little pieces of celery, with the white top attached, make also a pretty garnish. These sandwiches are not covered with a second slice of bread.

DEVILED SANDWICHES

Chop a quarter of a pound of cold, boiled tongue very fine; add to it two tablespoonfuls of olive oil, a dash of red pepper, a teaspoonful of Worcestershire sauce, and a saltspoonful of paprika; mix and add the hard-boiled yolks of three eggs that have been pressed through a sieve. Put this between thin slices of bread and butter, and garnish with water cress.

EGG SANDWICHES NO. 1

Take the hard-boiled yolks of six eggs and rub them to a paste, adding gradually two tablespoonfuls of olive oil or thick cream. Add a dash of paprika, one-half teaspoonful of salt, spread and finish precisely the same as tongue sandwich.

EGG SANDWICHES NO. 2

Put thin slices of hard-boiled eggs between slices of brown bread and butter; dust the egg slightly with salt and pepper. Trim the edges of the sandwiches with either cress or lettuce, and cut into triangles or squares.

FISH SANDWICHES

Rub to a smooth paste a quarter of a pound of cold, boiled fish; add half a teaspoonful of Worcestershire sauce, a tablespoonful of olive oil, a half saltspoonful of salt, and a half saltspoonful of black pepper. Spread the slices of bread on the loaf, cut them off about a half inch in thickness; trim off the crusts, put on each slice dainty lettuce leaves, and fill the center with the fish mixture. Cover with another layer of buttered bread from which you have trimmed the crusts, and press the two together.

FLAKED FISH SANDWICHES

Flake cold boiled white fleshed fish, dust it with salt and pepper and sprinkle it with lemon juice. Butter thin slices of brown bread; do not trim off the crusts. Put on one slice a layer of thin crisp cucumber, cover this with flaked fish, put a tablespoonful of mayonnaise in the center, put on another layer of chopped cress, then a slice of buttered brown bread. Press together and cut into halves.

SPANISH SANDWICHES

Mash the hard-boiled yolks of three eggs, add twelve boiled shrimps, either pounded in a mortar or chopped very fine. Add three tablespoonfuls of olive oil or butter, a tablespoonful of tomato catsup, two saltspoonfuls of paprika, four tablespoonfuls of chopped parsley, a half teaspoonful of salt, and at last stir in four tablespoonfuls of mayonnaise dressing. Spread this between thin slices of buttered bread, trim the crusts and cut into shape.

SALMON SANDWICHES

Flake cold boiled salmon, or open a can of salmon, drain it free from oil and break the fish apart in good-sized flakes; sprinkle them with salt, pepper and lemon juice. Butter slices of whole wheat or brown bread, cover with a layer of the salmon, then a thick layer of chopped cress or shredded celery. Put a tablespoonful of mayonnaise in the middle and cover with another slice of buttered bread. Press together, trim the crusts and cut into triangles.

SWEDISH SANDWICHES

Flake any cold cooked fish, dust it with salt, pepper and lemon juice. Rub the bottom of a bowl with a clove of garlic, add a half cupful of mayonnaise, four finely chopped gherkins, twelve chopped olives and two tablespoonfuls of capers. Mix and stir in two tablespoonfuls of finely chopped parsley. Spread a thin layer of this dressing over a plain slice of bread, do not butter the bread, cover it with fish, put on top a crisp lettuce leaf, then cover with another slice of bread that has been spread with the dressing. Press, trim the crusts and cut into fingers.

FRENCH CHICKEN SANDWICHES

Chop the white meat of one chicken very fine; pound to a paste. Add one-half teaspoonful of salt and a dash of red pepper. Cover one tablespoonful of gelatin, with a tablespoonful of cold water, soak it for about five minutes, then add to it ten tablespoonfuls of thick cream; stand this over teakettle and stir until gelatin is dissolved. Now, beat into this the chicken, stand it aside in a square pan until cold. Cut the chicken into very thin slices; put a slice on a slice of buttered bread; cover this with another slice of bread and cut into shape.

GAME SANDWICHES

Remove the breasts from two partridges after they have been baked or roasted. Chop the meat rather fine; reduce two sardines to a paste. While you are mashing the sardines, add gradually about two tablespoonfuls of soft butter, a dash of red pepper and a half teaspoonful of salt. Spread the bread first with the sardine paste; then sprinkle over the chopped game; dust this with salt and a little pepper; cover with another slice of bread, press lightly; trim into shape.

GERMAN SANDWICHES

Cut thin slices of rye bread; butter before you take them from the loaf. Spread each slice with a thin layer of limburger cheese. Cut bologna sausage into the thinnest possible slices; cover the limburger with the sliced bologna, and then a thin piece of pumpernickel; cover with another slice of bread that has been coated with a layer of cheese. Press the two together; do not remove the crusts. Serve on a napkin in a wicker basket.

HAM SANDWICHES

Chop cold boiled ham very fine. To each cupful of this ham, after it has been chopped, stir in two tablespoonfuls of melted butter, dash of red pepper and about one-half teaspoonful of onion juice. Have bread sufficiently stale to cut nicely. Remove end crust, butter and cut a very thin slice; remove the crusts, and spread with the ham paste. Serve same as tongue sandwiches.

INDIAN SANDWICHES

Take two sardines, remove skin and bones, put them into mortar and pound fine; add a teaspoonful of anchovy paste, a dash of salt and red pepper and the hard-boiled yolks of six eggs, rubbed smooth; stir two tablespoonfuls of olive oil into the mixture at the last. Cut bread into slices about half an inch thick, remove crusts, then cut into crescent-shaped pieces, toast, butter and cover with the mixture, serve at once.

LETTUCE SANDWICHES

Have bread made into a large, square loaf, take off the crust from one end, butter and then cut into slices. Take the white part of lettuce, wash and wipe it perfectly dry; have ready three hard-boiled eggs, remove the yolks, put them through a sieve and rub to a perfectly smooth paste with four tablespoonfuls of very thick cream. Add one-half tablespoonful lemon juice and then stir in about four tablespoonfuls of whipped cream; season with red pepper and add teaspoonful of salt. Cover slices of bread with leaves of lettuce, put on a goodly quantity of dressing and then on top of this another slice of bread. This may be served in squares tied together with ribbon, or they may be pressed and cut into long narrow pieces. Of course, they must be made only a short time before serving.

LOBSTER SANDWICHES

Whole wheat bread or the ordinary Boston brown bread is the most desirable for these sandwiches. Plunge the lobster into hot water; bring to boiling point, and simmer gently three-quarters of an hour; remove the meat, and cut it with a silver knife into dice. Now, sprinkle the lobster with a little salt, red pepper and a tablespoonful of tarragon vinegar. Allow it to stand for a few minutes, and then sprinkle over two or three tablespoonfuls of melted butter. As soon as the butter has chilled on the lobster, put a goodly layer over a slice of buttered bread; cover with another slice of bread; press the two together, and remove the crusts. Remember, there is only one layer of lobster between two slices of bread.

LOBSTER SALAD SANDWICHES

Cut fine the solid portion from one boiled lobster, put it into a bowl, dust it lightly with salt and pepper and sprinkle over two tablespoonfuls of lemon juice. Make a half cupful of mayonnaise from the yolk of one egg and eight tablespoonfuls of olive oil. Select crisp lettuce leaves. Mix the mayonnaise with the lobster, put a thin layer over a slice of buttered bread, cover with a lettuce leaf, put another thin layer of lobster on top of the lettuce leaf, then a second slice of buttered bread. Press firmly together, cut off the crusts and cut the slices into halves long ways, or you may make it into three fingers.

MUTTON SANDWICHES

Chop a half pound of cold, cooked mutton very fine; add two tablespoonfuls of cream or olive oil, a tablespoonful of capers, half a teaspoonful of salt, and a saltspoonful of pepper; mix thoroughly. Butter the slices on the loaf; cut them one-half inch thick, and trim off the crusts. Spread thickly with the mixture; put at each of the four corners a mint leaf; put on top another slice of buttered bread, from which you have trimmed the crust, press the two together, and cut from corner to corner making four triangles.

These sandwiches may also be flavored with tomato catsup.

MUTTON CLUB SANDWICHES

Cut brown bread into rounds or circles with an ordinary cake cutter. Chop one-half pound of cold, boiled mutton rather fine; add two tablespoonfuls of olive oil, half a teaspoonful of salt, and a saltspoonful of paprika. Peel four or five quite solid tomatoes, cut them into slices and push out the seeds. Put a slice of tomato on top of a round of bread, fill the space from which you have taken the seeds with the mutton mixture; put on top another round of buttered bread, and press the two together. You may, if you like, put on top of the tomato a lettuce leaf, and in the center of that half a teaspoonful of mayonnaise dressing. Nice for luncheon on a warm day.

ENGLISH MUTTON SANDWICHES

Chop sufficient cold boiled mutton to make a pint. Add to it two tablespoonfuls of capers, a half teaspoonful of salt, six tablespoonfuls of cream or olive oil and a saltspoonful of pepper. Mash carefully and put between layers of buttered bread; trim the crusts and cut into triangles.

SPRING LAMB SANDWICHES

Grind sufficient lamb to make a half pint, putting through the meat grinder with the lamb the leaves from six stalks of mint. Add a half teaspoonful of salt, two tablespoonfuls of melted butter or cream, and a saltspoonful of pepper. Rub this to a paste and spread between toasted English muffins. Leaves of mint may be put over the top of the lamb before putting the muffins together.

TURKISH SANDWICHES

Chop sufficient cold roasted mutton to make a pint; add two solid tomatoes from a can of tomatoes, or two fresh tomatoes, peeled, the seeds pressed out and the flesh chopped fine. Add a half cupful of piñons or pine nuts, and sufficient olive oil to bind the whole together. Spread this between thin, warm milk or beaten biscuits and serve for afternoon tea or supper.

PICNIC SANDWICHES

Take the ordinary French rolls; make a round opening in the top of each, and then, with your finger, scoop out all the crumb, leaving the roll in shape with a very small opening on top. Save the little piece of crust from the top of the opening. Mix together four olives, one gherkin, a tablespoonful of capers and one large green, sweet pepper, chopped very fine. Chop fine two ounces of tongue, and mix it with the white meat of one chicken, chopped fine. Mix together, and moisten with a well-made mayonnaise dressing. Fill this into the roll, put on the top, and arrange neatly on a napkin in a wicker basket; serve at once. The rolls may be prepared and the mixture made some time before serving, but the two should be put together at the last moment.

POTATO SANDWICHES

Mash four good-sized boiled potatoes; add a level teaspoonful of salt, four tablespoonfuls of thick cream, and the yolks of four hard-boiled eggs rubbed to a smooth paste, a saltspoonful of pepper, two tablespoonfuls of olive oil; mix thoroughly until you have a perfectly smooth paste. Put this between slices of brown bread and butter, trim off the crusts, and cut into triangles. The top may be garnished with cress or lettuce.

SALAD SANDWICHES

Chop fine half a pound of cold, cooked chicken; mix with it six tablespoonfuls of mayonnaise dressing; add half a teaspoonful of salt and a saltspoonful of pepper; put this between slices of bread and butter, and cut into fancy shapes.

These sandwiches may also be trimmed with lettuce or cress, and almost any meat may be substituted for the chicken. If beef is used, a tablespoonful of tomato catsup may be added; with mutton a tablespoonful of capers. Beef is much better garnished with cress, mutton with mint, chicken with lettuce or celery.

Lobsters and crabs may be mixed with mayonnaise and used as a salad sandwich; garnish of course with lettuce.

FISH SALAD SANDWICHES

Flake one can of salmon, or an equal quantity of cold boiled fish. Add to it a half teaspoonful of salt, a dash of cayenne and one ordinary cucumber, grated and drained. Just before serving time butter the bread, cut it into thin slices, put over the top a layer of the flaked fish, then a thin layer of mayonnaise or sandwich dressing and another covering of bread. Press together, trim the crusts and cut directly across the slice, making two long sandwiches about an inch and a half to two inches wide.

SARDINE SALAD SANDWICHES

These, like salmon sandwiches, are made from materials usually in every household, and can be made at a moment's notice. Stir four tablespoonfuls of oil into an egg, add a few drops of vinegar or lemon juice. Remove the sardines from the oil, take off the tails and heads and remove the bones. Mash them in a bowl, add a tablespoonful of vinegar, or the same amount of lemon juice. If you have lettuce or cress, either shred it, or put one leaf between the fish and the buttered bread.

SARDINE SANDWICHES

Cut slices of bread about one-half an inch thick, butter and toast; trim off the crust. Remove skin and bones from the sardines, lay them carefully over toast; have ready, chopped very fine, some olives and capers, mixed together; sprinkle these over the sardines, then a teaspoonful of lemon juice to each sandwich. Cut into any shape you may desire and they are ready to serve.

SWISS SANDWICHES

Put half a pound of ordinary schmierkase into a bowl, rub it perfectly smooth; add, a teaspoonful at a time, four tablespoonfuls of thick cream, two tablespoonfuls of melted butter, half a teaspoonful of salt, and a saltspoonful of pepper. Butter the slices of bread on the loaf; cut each off about a half inch in thickness, trim off the crusts and spread with the cheese mixture; put on top a layer of pumpernickel or rye bread; on top of that another thin layer of cheese, and on top of that another layer of white bread and butter; press these lightly together. If the crusts have been trimmed off, cut the slices into three or four finger shaped sandwiches. They should be the length of the slice and about one inch wide. These are exceedingly nice garnished with cress.

In arranging them for serving, put a layer of sandwiches and a layer of cress all through the basket or dish.

TONGUE SANDWICHES

Chop cold boiled tongue very fine. To each cupful stir in two tablespoonfuls of melted butter, dash of red pepper and about one-half teaspoonful of onion juice. Have bread sufficiently stale to cut nicely. Remove end crust, butter and cut a very thin slice; remove the crusts. Spread it with the tongue paste, roll each sandwich carefully, tie with narrow ribbon and put away until wanted. These can be made several hours before serving.

SANDWICH DRESSING

Put four tablespoonfuls of vinegar and three of water into a saucepan over the fire; add a half teaspoonful of salt and a half saltspoonful of pepper. Beat the yolks of four eggs until creamy, add slowly to them the hot mixture. Stir over hot water until it is the consistency of mayonnaise dressing. Take from the fire and add carefully two level tablespoonfuls of butter.

FARMER'S SANDWICHES

Butter each slice on the loaf, slice it off very thin. Remove the crusts, lay a crisp lettuce leaf on one half the buttered slices, spread with sandwich dressing and cover with a slice of buttered bread. Press the two together and cut into triangles. Cress, Romaine, or bleached chicory may be used in place of lettuce. These are more appetizing than ordinary bread and butter sandwiches, and are made from materials found in every household.

FARMER'S EGG SANDWICHES

Put six eggs into warm water, bring to a boil and keep at boiling point, without boiling hard, for a half hour. Throw them into cold water, remove the shells and cut them into slices lengthwise. A very fine wire is best for cutting eggs. Butter the slices on the loaf, then cut them off, cover with slices of hard-boiled eggs, dust lightly with salt and pepper. Spread the eggs carefully with sandwich dressing, put on another slice of buttered bread, press the two together and cut into triangles. If you have lettuce or cress put a leaf over the dressing.

DEVILED BEEF SANDWICHES

Chop remains of cold cooked beef very fine. To each pint add one tablespoonful of tomato catsup, a dash of cayenne, two tablespoonfuls of melted butter, a teaspoonful of Worcestershire sauce, a half teaspoonful of paprika and a tablespoonful of onion juice. Rub to a paste and put between thin slices of buttered bread, trim off the crusts and cut into triangles.

CORNED BEEF SANDWICHES

Chop sufficient cold cooked corned beef to make a pint. Add to it a teaspoonful of horseradish, four tablespoonfuls of melted butter or olive oil and four or five tablespoonfuls of finely-shredded water cress. Put this between slices of buttered whole wheat or brown bread; trim the crusts and cut into triangles.

PLAIN CORNED BEEF SANDWICHES

Butter an equal quantity of white and whole wheat bread. Cut the cooked corned beef into very thin slices. Put a slice on a slice of buttered bread, put on top a teaspoonful of creamed horseradish sauce, spread it out, cover with cress leaves, or crisp lettuce leaf, put on a slice of whole wheat bread, press the two together, trim the crusts and cut into fingers about one inch wide.

To make the creamed horseradish sauce, stir thick, dry whipped cream into dry horseradish. If the horseradish is in vinegar, press out the vinegar and then fold in the whipped cream.

SANDWICHES À LA STANLEY

Cut cold beef loaf or roll into very thin slices. Bake three or four bananas, and make a creamed horseradish sauce according to preceding recipe. Butter white or whole wheat bread, put on first a slice of meat, then just a thin layer of the mashed baked banana, then a teaspoonful of horseradish sauce, and another slice of bread. Press together, trim the crusts, cut into triangles and serve. These sandwiches should be served soon after they are made.

ENGLISH SALT-BEEF SANDWICHES

Whip a half cupful of cream until it is very stiff. Put four tablespoonfuls of freshly grated horseradish or horseradish pressed free from vinegar into a bowl, add the yolk of an egg and a saltspoonful of salt; mix and fold in the whipped cream. Have ready very thin slices of cold boiled salt beef. Butter thin slices of bread, put on a layer of salt beef, then a thin layer of the horseradish sauce and another layer of buttered bread. Press together, trim the crusts and cut into triangles.

SANDWICHES À LA BERNHARDT

Chop sufficient very rare cold roasted beef to make a half pint; mix with it a dash of cayenne, a half teaspoonful of salt, a tablespoonful of tomato catsup, a tablespoonful of mango chutney, two shallots, a half clove of garlic and a table-spoonful of olive oil. Spread this on a thin slice of buttered brown bread, cover it with leaves of cress, and then put on another thin slice of buttered white bread. Press the two together, cut into crescents or triangles.

EAST INDIAN LENTIL SANDWICHES

Take any left-over boiled or stewed lentils and press them through a sieve. To each half cupful of this mixture add a half cupful of chopped pecans, a level teaspoonful of curry and a saltspoonful of salt. Spread thin slices of brown bread with butter, then put over a thick layer of this mixture and cover with chopped parsley. Cover with another layer of brown bread, press together, trim the crusts and cut into fingers.

NUT-BUTTER SANDWICHES

Mix one glass of nut butter with two tablespoonfuls of olive oil and one ta-blespoonful of chopped pimientos. Spread this on a slice of unbuttered brown bread, cover with finely-chopped cress or shredded lettuce, place on top a slice of buttered bread, press the two together, trim the crusts and cut into fingers an inch wide.

FILIPINO SANDWICHES

Add one grated pineapple to a tumbler of peanut butter, mix thoroughly, add a tablespoonful of lemon juice, a dash of cayenne, a half teaspoonful of paprika. Put this between thin slices of brown bread, buttered; press together and cut into halves.

SWEET SANDWICHES

Under this heading we place all those dainty sandwiches that are made from thin slices of bread and butter and a jam or fruit filling. They are usually cut into circles; it is more economical to do this before the bread is buttered, unless you can cut rounds from one side, and a crescent above it. Almost any sweet may be used. Serve with chocolate or coffee according to the fruit, either for an afternoon tea or an "evening."

CHERRY SANDWICHES

Chop a quarter of a pound of candied cherries very fine, adding occasionally as you chop them a few drops of orange juice, if you use wine, a few drops of sherry. Mix thoroughly and spread over water thins, making it a little deeper in the center than at the edges. These sandwiches are better made from crackers than from bread. Arrange neatly on a pretty glass dish, and they are ready to serve.

FIG SANDWICHES

Split a dozen figs and scrape out the soft portion, rejecting the skins; work this to a paste. Cut the slices of bread from the loaf, buttering before you cut them; make them quite thin. Remove the crusts, and spread this thick paste over the bread and roll carefully; press for a moment until there is no danger of the roll opening; roll each in a piece of tissue paper; twist the ends as you would an old-fashioned "secret," or they may be tied with baby ribbon. These are exceedingly wholesome and palatable.

FRUIT AND NUT SANDWICHES

These are perhaps the most attractive of all the sweet sandwiches.

Put through the meat chopper a quarter of a pound of almonds with half a pound of washed figs, the same quantity of dates, the same of raisins, and a pound of pecan nuts; put them through alternately so that they will be mixed in chopping. Pack the mixture into round baking powder tins, pressing it down firmly, and stand it aside over night. When wanted, dip the tin in hot water, loosen it with a knife and shake out the mixture. With a sharp knife cut into very thin slices and put them between two rounds of buttered bread. Serve with chocolate.

The combination may be varied; candied cherries, citron or any of the candied fruits may be substituted for the dates and figs. Brazilian and pine nuts may be substituted for a portion of the pecans.

ORANGE MARMALADE SANDWICHES

These sandwiches may be made precisely the same as fig sandwiches, substituting the orange marmalade for the figs.

SPONGE CAKE SANDWICHES

Bake a sponge cake in a square loaf; cut it into slices a quarter of an inch thick; cut the slices into rounds with a small biscuit cutter. With another small cutter take out the center leaving the ring; put this ring on top of a solid round making sort of a patty as it were; fill the spaces with a mixture of chopped candied fruit that has been soaked in orange juice over night; cover the top with the meringue made from white of egg and sugar; put them in the oven to brown, dish neatly and they are ready to use. These cannot stand over an hour as the fruit will soften the cake.

FRESH FRUIT SANDWICHES

These sandwiches are exceedingly nice to serve for afternoon teas. They must be used soon after they are made. They will, however, if wrapped in a damp napkin, keep for an hour, but as fruit is soft the bread is liable to become moist, which spoils the sandwich.

Butter the bread and put between layers of sliced strawberries, dusted with powdered sugar; or raspberries, or large blackberries cut into halves; or peaches, finely chopped; or apple seasoned with a little salt, pepper, olive oil and lemon juice; or sliced bananas with a dash of lemon juice, are all nice.

RAISIN SANDWICHES

Put one-half pound of seeded raisins through the meat grinder, add a quarter of a pound of almonds that have been blanched, dried and ground. Add a half tumbler of quince jelly, mix thoroughly and put between thin slices of buttered white bread. These sandwiches are very nice in place of cake for afternoon teas or evening companies.

AFTERNOON TEAS

Stone a quarter of a pound of dates, put them through a meat grinder, add to them a half tumbler of nut butter, mix until smooth, add four tablespoonfuls of sweet cream and a tablespoonful of orange juice. Put this mixture between thin slices of white buttered bread, press together, trim the crusts and cut into fingers or four small triangles.

NUT AND APPLE SANDWICHES

Put a half cupful of *thick* stewed apples into a bowl, add the grated yellow rind of quarter of an orange and one cupful of finely chopped mixed nuts. Spread this on saltines, Uneedas, or any crisp cracker. Put on top another cracker and serve at once. These are very nice for children's parties. Of course one may use buttered bread, either white or brown.

GRAPE FRUIT SANDWICHES

Spread any crisp cracker with a thin layer of grape fruit marmalade, put on top another cracker and serve at once.

GINGER SANDWICHES

Put four or five pieces of ginger through your meat chopper. Stir this paste into a half cupful of orange marmalade. Put between slices of buttered bread, press them together, trim the crusts and cut into fingers. These are nice for afternoon teas. Ginger and carrot marmalade are also very nice.

CANAPÉS

These are slices of bread cut into fancy shapes, toasted or quickly fried in hot oil, or they may be spread with butter and browned in a quick oven. One slice only is used for each canapé. The mixture is spread on top, the top garnished, and the canapé used at once.

ANCHOVY CANAPÉS

Cover a round or square of toast with anchovies that have been mashed and seasoned with a little tomato catsup. Put a little chopped celery around the edge as a garnish and send at once to the table.

CAVIAR CANAPÉS

Season the caviar with onion and a very little lemon juice; spread over a round or square canapé, put chopped onion around the edge, garnish the top with a hard-boiled egg; place on paper mats and send at once to the table. These are used as first course at lunch or dinner.

SWEDISH CANAPES

Cut thick slices of whole wheat or Graham bread, trim the crusts and hollow out the centers, being careful not to make a hole all the way through. Pound or mash the hard boiled yolks of three eggs with a tablespoonful of anchovy paste or two anchovies, two tablespoonfuls of butter and a dash of lemon juice. Cut a dill pickle lengthwise into slices an eighth of an inch thick, then cut these slices into long strips a half inch wide. Cut large pickled beets into strips of the same width. Cut a dozen pimolas into halves. Butter the bread, fill with the paste, put over the strips of dill pickle, leaving one inch between each strip. Cross these with strips of pickled beets, put half of a pimola into each square. Dish on paper mats. Serve as an appetizer before soup.

CHOPPED TONGUE CANAPÉS

Chop cold, cooked tongue very fine; season it with two tablespoonfuls of olive oil and a dusting of pepper; spread it over the top of a round of toasted bread; garnish the edge with the small leaves of cress, put a little grated hard-boiled egg in the center and send at once to the table.

SARDINE CANAPÉS

Remove the skin and pound the sardines to a paste; put a thick layer of this paste over the top of a round of toasted bread. Cut one gherkin into very thin slices, arrange them overlapping around the edge; put a little finely chopped hard-boiled egg in the center, and they are ready to serve.

FISH CANAPÉS

Pound a quarter of a pound of cooked fish to a paste; season it with a few drops of onion juice, a saltspoonful of salt, and a dash of black pepper. Stir into it two tablespoonfuls of sauce tartare; spread this on six or eight rounds of buttered bread browned in the oven; garnish the tops with grated cucumber and send to the table.

DEVILED OYSTER CANAPÉS

Cut slices of bread into squares, toast and remove the crusts. Remove the hard part from a pint of pickled oysters, place oysters over bread, close together and in rotation, dust thickly with red pepper; put over as a thin covering a highly seasoned sauce mayonnaise, and serve. Do not put over a second piece of bread.

PÂTÉ DE FOIE GRAS CANAPÉS

For twenty-four sandwiches take one tureen of foie gras. Remove the fat, and mash the foie gras to a perfectly smooth paste, adding gradually four tablespoon-fuls of soft, not melted, butter; add a dash of cayenne and a half teaspoonful of salt and about ten drops of onion juice, and press the whole through a sieve. Cut slices of bread into fancy shapes and toast; crescents are very pretty. Cover each slice thickly with this paste; garnish with hard-boiled white of egg, cut into diamonds or tiny crescents, and olives cut into rings. Arrange neatly, and they are ready to serve.

HOT CANAPÉS

A canapé is the half of a sandwich, as it were. Minced meats of various kinds are served on one slice of bread. In many books they are called "uncovered sand-wiches." The cold canapés are placed always among the appetizers and served before the soup. They are made of such materials as caviar, sardines, anchovies, pickled oysters, pickled lobster, deviled shrimps, or a mixture of one or two of these materials.

A hot canapé, however, is served in the place of fish or as an entrée. If they are dressed with either fish or shell-fish they will take the place of that course. When made from chicken, sweetbreads or game, should be served as an entrée, follow-ing the fish.

FISH CANAPÉS

Pick apart sufficient cold cooked fish to make a half pint. Rub together two level tablespoonfuls of butter and two of flour, add a half pint of milk, stir until boiling, add a half teaspoonful of salt, a teaspoonful of soy, a dash of red pepper and a half saltspoonful of black pepper. When this is hot add the fish and four or five nice sliced mushrooms; stand over hot water, without stirring, until the fish is thoroughly heated. While this is heating, trim the crusts from six slices of bread; toast the one side carefully. Have ready in your pastry bag with a star tube a pint of light mashed potatoes; press in a rope-like form, or in small rosettes, around the edge of the bread on the untoasted side. Brush the bread with a little melted butter, put them in the oven until the potatoes and bread are a golden brown. Dish these on square paper mats on individual plates, fill the centers with the creamed fish and send at once to the table.

Canned salmon may be used in the place of fresh boiled fish.

LOBSTER CANAPÉS

    1 three-pound lobster
    The yolks of two eggs
    2 level tablespoonfuls of butter
    2 level tablespoonfuls of flour
    ½ pint of milk
    1 tablespoonful of chopped parsley
    1 level teaspoonful of salt
    1 saltspoonful of white pepper
    1 pint of mashed potatoes
    6 slices of bread

Toast the bread and arrange the potatoes according to the preceding recipe. Rub the butter and flour together, add the milk; when boiling add the seasoning and the lobster. When very hot stir in carefully the well-beaten yolks of the eggs. Stir this until it is smoking hot, but be careful not to boil, or it will curdle. Fill this on top of the toast that has been garnished with potatoes, dust with chopped parsley and send to the table.

Shrimps may be substituted for lobster.

SWEETBREAD CANAPÉS

    1 pair calf's sweetbreads
    ½ can of mushrooms
    2 level tablespoonfuls of butter
    2 level tablespoonfuls of flour
    ½ pint of milk
    ½ teaspoonful of salt
    1 saltspoonful of pepper

Boil the sweetbreads carefully for three-quarters of an hour; throw them into cold water; pick them apart, rejecting the membrane. Chop the mushrooms very fine, add them to the sweetbreads. Rub the butter and flour together, add the milk; when boiling add the salt, pepper, sweetbreads and mushrooms; cover and stand over hot water ten to fifteen minutes. Serve them on slices of bread, garnished with mashed potatoes pressed through a star tube.

CANAPÉS À LA TRINIDAD

Half the white meat from one boiled chicken
1 pair of sweetbreads
6 large fresh mushrooms
2 level tablespoonfuls of butter
2 level tablespoonfuls of flour
½ pint of milk
2 yolks of hard-boiled eggs
1 level teaspoonful of salt
1 saltspoonful of pepper

Cut twelve slices of bread; trim the crusts so the slices will be of even size. Cut out the centers from one-half the slices, leaving a wall of one inch. Toast the solid slices. Brush the untoasted edge of the bread with a little white of egg, lay on the rims and put them in the oven to toast on the upper side. Pick the sweetbreads apart, after they are carefully cooked, rejecting the membrane. Slice the mushrooms. Cut the chicken into dice. Put the butter into a saucepan, add the mushrooms, toss for a minute until the mushrooms are slightly softened, then add the flour, mix, and add the milk, salt and pepper. Cover this on the back part of the stove for ten or fifteen minutes until the mushrooms are cooked; then add the meat. Stand this over hot water ten or fifteen minutes. The toast should now be done and crisp. Arrange each canapé on a square of lace paper on an individual heated dish, put the mixture in the center, garnish with the yolk of the eggs pressed through a sieve. Garnish the very top with a little chopped truffle or a little chopped parsley. These are the handsomest of all hot canapés, and while they are usually served following the soup at dinner, they may be used for the main course at a ladies' luncheon, or at a supper.

GAME CANAPÉS

Cut any pieces of left-over game into dice. Put two tablespoonfuls of butter and two of flour in a saucepan, add a half pint of stock. When boiling add a half can of very fine mushrooms, a tablespoonful of chopped ham, a tablespoonful of chopped parsley, a level teaspoonful of salt and a saltspoonful of pepper. Bring this to a boil, add the game; stand over hot water for fifteen or twenty minutes until the game has absorbed part of the sauce, then add two tablespoonfuls of sherry or Madeira, and fill into the square canapés made the same as in preceding recipe.

LAMB CANAPÉS

2 cans, or one quart of cooked peas
1 blade of mace
2 level tablespoonfuls of butter
2 level tablespoonfuls of flour
½ pint of stock
1 teaspoonful of kitchen bouquet
½ teaspoonful of salt
1 tablespoonful of chopped onion

2 tablespoonfuls of claret
1 saltspoonful of pepper

Put the butter and onion in a saucepan, shake it over the fire, then add the cold boiled lamb, cut into blocks; you should have one pint. When this is boiling add all the seasoning and stand the mixture over hot water on the back of the stove while you make the canapés. Press the peas through a sieve; the pulp must be quite dry; add to it a palatable seasoning of salt and pepper and one or two tablespoonfuls of melted butter. Put these in a pastry bag. Toast the bread on one side, put the peas around in rope-like form, or roses, on the untoasted side, making a border sufficiently high to hold the lamb. Stand in the oven until the bread is carefully toasted. Arrange them on lace papers on heated plates, fill the center with the lamb mixture and send to the table.

CLUB-HOUSE SANDWICHES

Club-house sandwiches may be made in a number of different ways, but are served warm as a rule on bread carefully toasted at the last moment. Put on top of a square of toasted bread a thin layer of broiled ham or bacon; on top of this a thin slice of Holland pickle, on top of that a thin slice of cold roasted chicken or turkey, then a leaf of lettuce in the center of which you put a teaspoonful of mayonnaise dressing; cover this with another slice of buttered toast. Press the two together, and cut from one corner to another making two large triangles, and send at once to the table.

People not using ham may make a palatable sandwich by putting down first a layer of cold boiled tongue, then a layer of Holland cucumber, a layer of turkey or chicken, another layer of cucumber and the slice of toast. Garnish with little pieces of water cress before putting on the last slice.

SCENTED SANDWICHES

There is a group of rather æsthetic sandwiches made from thin slices of bread and butter flavored or scented with flowers. Among those in common use are clover, rose and the nasturtium.

The crust is trimmed off from the outside of the loaf; the loaf placed down in a clean stone jar in a nest of clover blossoms; the butter is put in a piece of cheese cloth and also covered with clover, and the jar covered over night. The next morning the bread and butter will have the flavor of clover.

ROSE SANDWICHES

In making rose sandwiches cover the bread and butter with rose leaves over night. Put a few rose petals between the slices when making the sandwiches.

NASTURTIUM SANDWICHES

Cover the bread and butter with nasturtium flowers over night. In making the sandwiches place at each corner of the slice a flower, so that in cutting from corner to corner you have a little triangular sandwich holding a nasturtium flower uncut.

VIOLET SANDWICHES

These are made the same, covering the slice of bread and butter with the petals of the violet.

Lector House believes that a society develops through a two-fold approach of continuous learning and adaptation, which is derived from the study of classic literary works spread across the historic timeline of literature records. Therefore, we aim at reviving, repairing and redeveloping all those inaccessible or damaged but historically as well as culturally important literature across subjects so that the future generations may have an opportunity to study and learn from past works to embark upon a journey of creating a better future.

This book is a result of an effort made by Lector House towards making a contribution to the preservation and repair of original ancient works which might hold historical significance to the approach of continuous learning across subjects.

HAPPY READING & LEARNING!

LECTOR HOUSE LLP
E-MAIL: lectorpublishing@gmail.com

www.ingramcontent.com/pod-product-compliance
Lightning Source LLC
Chambersburg PA
CBHW051408130726
47987CB00007B/2899